IMAGES
of Ireland

EAST BELFAST

Campbell College, 1909. The College was founded from the bequest of Henry James Campbell, a flax and tow merchant. Designed in the Tudor Revivalist style by W.H. Lynn, it opened with 215 pupils on 3 September 1894 on the Belmont estate purchased from Sir Thomas McClure.

This book is dedicated to Victor Kelly

IMAGES
of Ireland

EAST BELFAST

Compiled by
Keith Haines
with the assistance of Wesley Thompson and Billy Bowden

First published 1997
Copyright © Keith Haines, 1997

Gill and Macmillan Publishers
Goldenbridge, Inchicore
Dublin 8

ISBN 0 7171 2644 7

Typesetting and origination by
Tempus Publishing Limited
Printed in Great Britain by
Midway Clark Printing, Wiltshire

Aerial view of East Belfast, 1962. The Albert Bridge can be seen to the west, and the Holywood Arches junction is at the top right of the view. The Castlereagh Road leads off to the lower right, with its main junction at Ladas Drive.

Contents

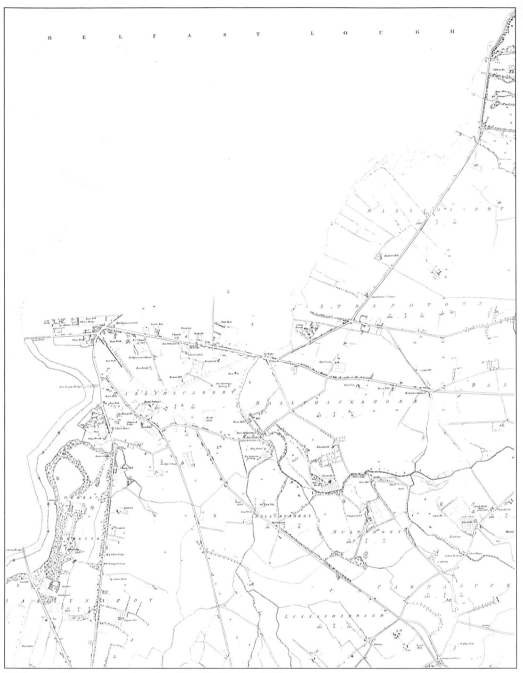

Ordnance Survey map showing East Belfast in 1838.

Introduction

The growth of East Belfast is rooted in the astonishing development of the townland of Ballymacarrett. Rev John Redmond, incumbent of Ballymacarrett Church of Ireland in the 1920s, observed that: 'In 1744 Ballymacarrett is described as containing only two buildings, Mountpottinger and a mill ... The village at the end of the [18th] century consisted of long rows of whitewashed cottages from Queen's Bridge to Connswater'; and yet the same author pointed out that about 150 years later Ballymacarrett – by then absorbed into the widening boundaries of the greater Belfast conurbation – was singularly as large as Londonderry.

As Victor Kelly, one of the founder members of the East Belfast Historical Society, and Trevor Carleton reiterated: 'Field after field formerly devoted to grazing ... has fallen to the avarice of the builders'. East Belfast grew apace from an intrinsically agricultural age at the close of the 18th century to dense urbanisation a century later.

Its expanding boundary has encompassed many contrasts. Built to accommodate a population migrating from the Ulster countryside, its serried terraces along such as the Newtownards Road and Short Strand – occasionally of such poor quality that their walls absorbed winter frosts and seepage from the Lagan – sat tidily but unprepossessingly in the shadow of the mansions of the industrialists and entrepreneurs at Knock, Strandtown and the appropriately-named Belmont.

Those ensnared by the poverty of a working-class existence saw the goods they manufactured dispersed along the transatlantic and imperial trade routes. Many of them met those who sailed

View of the River Lagan and Halfpenny Bridge, c. 1835, attributed to Hugh Fraser. The kilns of the glass works at the Long Bridge, shown on the Ordnance Survey map (*opposite*), can be seen in the distance. Halfpenny Bridge, so-called because it was a toll-bridge, has now been replaced by the Albert Bridge.

Sirocco Works, 1898.

into Belfast Lough from farther shores; served those – such as Davidson senior and junior of Sirocco Works – who had a broader vision and ventured around the world; and helped to construct the ships which navigated the world's oceans – or, as in the case of the *Titanic*, almost!

The more harmonious, if passionate, orchestrations of the ubiquitous bands have clamoured alongside the cacophony of shipyard, forge and factory machinery. Occasionally, the strains have proved more melodious, for it was within East Belfast that James Galway learned much about his craft.

The character of the people of East Belfast has been forged as much in the foundry of adversity as of its engineering shops. Economic depression has left its scars on both the environment and the inhabitants. There have been those who have not always comprehended. In the 1920s, one of the staff of Campbell College used to walk from the town centre to Belmont through the less salubrious streets of Ballymacarrett, and observed many of the unemployed leaning idly against public houses. 'How far better these men would be employed,' he suggested, 'had they some rational interest in life, some hobby ... or if they were to remain quietly at home and read some work of philosophy: Kant's *Critique of Pure Reason*, for example, or Dante's *Divine Comedy*'!

Few people of East Belfast are acquainted with Kant; equally as few would tolerate cant. They are a solid, resilient and self-reliant breed, and the Society hopes that these pages go some way towards reflecting this.

K. Haines
Hon. Sec., EBHS

One
Byways

McMaster Street, near the lower end of Newtownards Road, is a designated conservation area.

Holywood Arches, *c.* 1900. The left fork is Holywood Road, and the right leads to the Upper Newtownards Road. The bridge carried the Belfast & County Down Railway.

Following the closure of the Belfast & County Down Railway in 1948, the demolition of the Holywood Arches a few years later opened up a brighter prospect.

An idealised image of life at the Holywood Arches. Drawn by Thomas Clarke, this drawing depicts 'general dealer' Gusty Leebody. Leebody had a stabling yard at Scotch Row off Newtownards Road for twenty years up to the early 1970s.

Sirocco Tea makes full use of stationary and mobile advertising.

A pony and trap on Upper Newtownards Road, *c.* 1920.

The Glen at Belmont in the early part of the century. It does not look too different today.

Gelston's Corner, Belmont Road, towards the end of the First World War. Tedford's posting establishment, right, now The Stormont Inn, operated between 1905 and 1922, and Balmer's, left, from 1916. The building, now a cycle shop, was originally intended to be a hotel.

Belmont Road from Ranfurly Drive looking down towards the Holywood Road. This scene photographed about 1935 had not changed substantially since the time of the First World War.

White Row, Ravenhill Road. Mary McKibben and Isabella Sloan stand outside Carrie Dunn's (*see photograph on p. 65*). The row disappeared with road widening. Rowel Friers wrote in his autobiography: 'The white houses were much older than the dark brown ones and a lot smaller. A tall man could have touched the guttering should he have felt so inclined'.

Club Row, when it first appeared around 1870, was described as 'a few small houses'. This picture probably dates from the end of the 19th century.

Fraser Street before demolition at the end of the 1970s, looking towards St Matthew's Church on Newtownards Road (*see also photograph on p. 61*).

The demolition of 222 Albertbridge Road. The last principal occupant was Anna Campbell, a draper, who left in 1953. After two more years the property was never occupied again before its demolition in the late 1980s.

Queen's Bridge looking towards Ballymacarrett. Sirocco Works and the chimney of the glass kiln at Bridge End can be seen in the centre.

Newtownards Road, c. 1970. The tower belonged to the New Princess picture-house which operated from c. 1915 to the early 1960s. It became Stewart's supermarket in 1970.

Mountpottinger Corner, *c.* 1920. Charles Murray's Junction Arms was popularly called 'Holy Joe's'. Melville's, at the junction of Cluan Place, was a shrouding warehouse up to 1932, and the Picturedrome, built 1911, is beyond that. (UFTM: WAG 3824)

Mountpottinger Corner in the early years of this century. Adam Turner, right, was an undertaker on Albertbridge Road between 1904 and 1932. Davidson & Murray's (*see photograph on p. 67*) can be seen on the left.

Belmont Church Road, off Upper Newtownards Road, boasted some of the more affluent residences in the early decades of the twentieth century.

Conn O'Neill's Bridge, showing the river in flood at Connswater Street, 1905. The dating of this crossing has always proved very controversial.

The widening of North Road at the end of the 1920s.

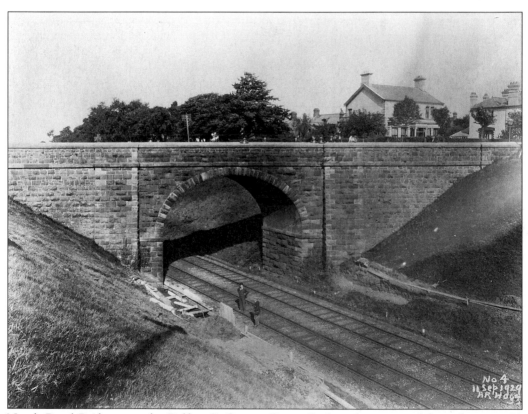

North Road Bridge over the Belfast & County Down Railway line, viewed from the east, 11 September 1929.

The old wooden footbridge across the Connswater river at Mersey Street was demolished at the end of the Second World War.

The first gable-end painting in Ulster dates back to 1908. The current Troubles, however, engendered much of the present artistic enterprise. This one appears in Severn Street, and has recently been renovated. The banner has been altered from its original: 'Their only crime was loyalty'.

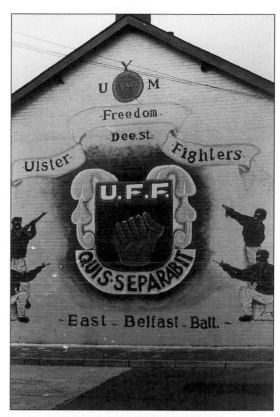

Two more wall paintings off Mersey Street.

Knock Road, Belfast

Knock Road, 1920s. Viewed from the junction with Upper Newtownards Road, Knock Methodist Church is visible in the distance.

Knock Road, 1997. Although the Knock Road has been considerably widened as part of the ring road, the view on the right has changed little in seventy years.

Two
People and Occasions

Collapse of the Halfpenny Bridge, 1886 (*see picture on p. 7*). This was to be replaced by the Albert Bridge in 1894. St John's Church, which was demolished in the mid-1950s, can be seen on the far left. The horse and carriage belongs to the photographer.

Sir Thomas McClure was a tobacco merchant and Liberal MP for Belfast. He popularised Ballymacarrett beaver hats, which were manufactured on Newtownards Road. He sold Belmont House to Campbell College in 1890.

The 'Twelfth', 1935. The parade on Belmont Road passes Clonallon House which had been owned by the Coates family. This house was destroyed by fire during the blitz of 4-5 May 1941. Two people were later killed in riots when this procession returned to the centre of Belfast.

Col. Wallace, the Marquis of Londonderry and Sir Edward Carson march to 'Craigavon' (*see photograph on p. 109*) on the 'Twelfth', 1913.

Part of the processions on the 'Twelfth', 1913, during the Home Rule crisis.

The 'Twelfth' at Glenwherry Street, probably at the turn of the century.

Bright Street Orange Arch, 1901. If the date of the photograph is correct, Stronge's tobacconist at 268 Newtownards Road, at the rear of the picture, had only just opened. (UFTM: L1261/4)

Locals gather under the Arch at the top of Sandown Road. Jubilee School, on the left, was built in 1846 and obtained its name in 1887 – Queen Victoria's Golden Jubilee year. It closed in 1930. The photograph was taken after 1912, for the Arch urges people to 'Remember the Covenant'.

The 'Twelfth' in Trillick Street, 1960s. In front of the banner stand, from left to right: Harry McAdams, Tom Ritchie and Andy McDowell. Alec McCarroll stands to the left of the lamp-post's shadow.

VE Day, 8 May 1945, in Roxburgh Street. An air-raid shelter can be seen to the left.

Another VE Day street party, probably in the Cregagh area.

ULSTER WELCOMES HER KING AND QUEEN

At the time of the royal visit to Ulster in 1937, a contest was held on Newtownards Road for the best arch. It seemed impossible to decide between Connswater Street (pictured) and Cable Street. However, closer inspection revealed that the square boxes shown (butter-butts) had been lightly painted, but it was still possible to read 'Made in Eire'. Cable Street was declared the winner!

39th Old Boys' Flute Band march on the 'Twelfth' during the 1950s. Gordon Titterington beats the drum on the left; far right is Davy Wright. The drum-major is Albert Stevens, and just behind his left shoulder Edmund Duke plays the flute.

Horatio Todd, chemist. From his pharmacy on Holywood Road (*see photograph on p. 62*), Todd created perfumes such as Marshmallow Linctus, in addition to producing his own conditioner and worm powders. He sent a selection of his 'Ulster Perfumes' to Buckingham Palace in 1925.

Four generations *c.* 1930. On the right: William Cully and his daughter Margaret Dunwoody. Her son William, left, was a mason, and was a founder member of the 39th Old Boys Flute Band (*see photograph on p. 30*). His young son, William junior, took over the reins of the 39th, was James Galway's first flute teacher, and was awarded the MBE for services to music in 1984.

James Galway amongst friends in East Belfast. From left to right: Elena Duran, Colin Fleming (principal flute of the Ulster Orchestra), Billy Dunwoody MBE, James Galway, Paddy Maloney (of The Chieftains) and Jeanne Galway.

Coronation Day 1953, Loopland Drive. From left to right, front row: Mrs Gregg, Mrs Richmond, Mrs Keary, Mrs Jackson, Mrs Minnie Rainey and Mrs Dalzell; back row: -?-, Mr Giboney (manager of the Cregagh Dairies), Mr Keary, Mrs Hazel Armstrong, Mr Dalzell, Mr and Mrs Tosh, -?-, Mrs Gartside and Mr Gregg.

Loopland Coronation children's party 1953. To the right, dressed in the flag, is Mrs Rainey, who owned a corner shop on the other side of the Castlereagh Road. To her right is her daughter, Mrs Armstrong.

HM The Queen, now the Queen Mother, followed by Princess Margaret, and accompanied by the Moderator of the General Assembly, Rev Dr John McKean, visits Campbell College on 1 June 1951 to present the Charter of Incorporation. Amongst the staff are: Bob Wells (to left with spectacles), Raoul Larmour (two to the left of the Queen) and, between the Princess and the Moderator, Kenneth Armour, one of the sons of the famous Rev J.B. Armour of Ballymoney.

St John Greer Ervine (1883-1971), playwright, novelist and biographer, was probably born in Isthmus Street (Woodstock Road), and educated at Westbourne School, Newtownards Road. He was later voted into the Irish Academy of Letters.

Four young members of Ballymacarrett Flute Band photographed at The Oval, 1920s.

C.S. Lewis at the age of six. He lived at 'Little Lea' on Circular Road, a home (*see photograph on p. 39*) which inspired his writing of *The Chronicles of Narnia*.

John and Daniel (on trike) Rodgers. The latter was killed during the Second World War when a bomb dropped on Hatton Drive (Woodstock Road). His mother, who had converted all her money into coins, suffered the additional indignity of having them sprayed all around!

The aircraft of 502 Ulster (Bombing) Squadron dip in salute at the foundation-stone-laying ceremony at Stormont, 19 May 1928.

The inspection of the Guard of Honour by HRH The Prince of Wales at the opening of the Stormont Parliament, 16 November 1932.

Hill & Craig workshops, Coronation Day, 1953. The man seated in the centre is Mr Jack Craig. Amongst the ladies on the left are Nellie Gibson, Meta Montgomery (now Lynar) and Isabelle Spence.

William Slator, principal of Strandtown National School (1898-1916) (*see also photograph on p. 81*). The boxes on the right appear to belong to the Great Northern Mineral Water Co., which was based at 59 Boundary Street.

Rev Canon Charles William Harding, born in Co. Offaly, was rector at Willowfield parish church (*see photograph on p. 83*) from 1900 to 1922. He showed much concern for the welfare of the working man and of children. He gave his name to Willowfield No 2 National School (*see photograph on p. 77*) which was called the Harding Memorial School after 1922.

10th Boy Scouts marching past Ballyhackamore House, *c.* 1910. The house stood off Holywood Road, above where the RUC station now stands.

Three

Homes

Reception hall to 'Little Lea', the childhood home of Oxford don, C.S. Lewis (*see photograph on p. 35*). The house on Circular Road was built by his father, Albert, for £400 and there were those who believed him to have been duped! The hall and fireplace are as Albert Lewis built them.

Belmont House. This estate gave the district its name. Built in the 1830s, it was originally the home of Alexander Montgomery, and later of Sir Thomas McClure (*see photograph on p. 24*) who sold the 70-acre estate in 1890 to the trustees of Henry James Campbell in order to found a school.

Between 1891 and 1894 Belmont House effectively became the clerk of works' office for the construction of Campbell College. The school was erected around the house, which was then demolished. It does not appear to have been particularly elegant.

Ormiston was built by a Scot, James Combe, in 1865 as a memorial to his father. It was allegedly constructed in Scotland, in the Scottish Baronial style, and then dismantled and shipped over to the estate in Belmont! It was owned amongst others by Sir Edward Harland and Lord Pirrie, until it was sold in 1927 to Campbell College. In 1974 it was acquired by the Police Authority, but is currently unoccupied.

Built around 1875 for the Robertson family, Netherleigh was purchased by Samuel Hall-Thompson in 1921. However, the linen trade became less profitable in the 1920s and he sold it to Campbell College. It is said that he encouraged the sale by threatening to sell it to the new Strathearn girls' school! Even in the late 1920s, however, its sanitation still involved the use of a cesspit.

Laxey House, Larkfield Road, Sydenham. Edward Armstrong and Sarah Armstrong, extreme right, at the time of their wedding, which took place in a registry office, at the end of the nineteenth century. Sarah Johnston stands between them.

Fountain Villas, Cherryvalley. The date on the house appears to be 1885.

Glenmachan Tower was designed in the 1860s by Thomas Jackson for Sir Thomas McClure. In recent years it was a hotel. The building is still in use.

Marietta House on Barnett's Road, off King's Road. From the end of the last century up to the close of the Second World War, the occupants included John Hanna, Thomas Sawers (the game, fish and poultry merchant), J.P. Mackie and R.H. Jackson.

'Homes fit for heroes', Somme estate, Cregagh. These houses were built for 36th (Ulster) Division soldiers returning from the front. The streets bear such names as Hamel Drive, Somme Drive and Thiepval Avenue.

This house on Church Road, Castlereagh – according to the misspelt plaque on its exterior wall – was 'Built by Robert Leathem, Anno Domoni [sic] 1768'.

When photographed in the 1930s, these old thatched cottages at Ballyhackamore were already in a state of dilapidation.

No 189 Albertbridge Road, on the corner of Templemore Avenue. Dating from the 1870s, it was owned between 1890 and the 1950s by Dr James Dunlop Williamson, once High Sheriff of Belfast; a crest bearing his initials and the date 1912 is visible between the upper-storey windows. It is now the surgery of Dr Breach and his daughter, Dr Christie.

No 94 Castlereagh Street dates from the 1880s and, despite its apparently modest size, was at the turn of the century the family home of John Kelly and his son (the future Sir) Samuel, who owned Kelly Coal. It is now a dentist's surgery and has been much modified since this earlier picture.

Some of the roofs in Castlereagh Street boasted some fine, decorative ironwork.

By the 1980s, 36 The Mount was the last large terraced house privately occupied. Its resident, probably pictured here, was Arthur Howard, a joiner. At the turn of the century the owner was James McQuoid, who had four sons. One was killed in the First World War; one went to Los Angeles, another (Louis) developed McQuoid's estate agency and the fourth, a barrister, became an assistant deputy commissioner in British West Africa.

Isa and Lucinda Millar outside 14 Newcastle Street 1940s. Polychrome brickwork was typical of the housing of the last twenty years of the nineteenth century.

Quasi-medieval decoration on the end house of Trillick Street (Beersbridge Road end).

Decorative face on a bay window at 103 The Mount, with the name Ava (relating to the Marquis of Dufferin & Ava, reason unknown) carved beneath it.

Probably because of the grimy working conditions, a number of houses sported foot-scrapers, as seen here in Glenmore Street.

Ashes were gathered from the hearth and placed in the yard by the ash-pit door, which could then be opened by those who did the rounds collecting the ashes.

21 Cluan Place (*see photograph on p. 17*), 1970s. In 1858 Cluan Place consisted of twelve houses off Mountpottinger Road. This block, in 'cottage style' – which consisted of projecting porch, tiny front garden with railings, and decorated with polychrome brickwork – and with a rear entrance, was added in 1887, and was eventually to back on to the Mountpottinger Tram Depot (*see photograph on p. 101*), constructed in the 1890s. Cluan Place was also to become the main access route to Musgrave's Foundry, built in 1893.

Four
Wartime

East Belfast Ulster Volunteer Force (UVF), 1912. Such units were formed to challenge the emerging threat of Home Rule. The recruits are pictured with members of the Royal Black Preceptory at the Dee Street 'Twelfth' Arch. It is not clear whether the rifles are replicas or genuine ones – Fred Crawford's gun-running at Larne did not occur until 1914. Many in the UVF were to volunteer in 1914 for the ranks of the 36th (Ulster) Division.

WELCH. 4

Campbell College was the first Irish school to form an officer training corps in early 1909. As a result of the training which they received, the vast majority of the 594 pupils who enlisted during the First World War were to be officers. Each year on Empire Day a tree was planted in the school grounds by the head prefect. Reginald Cuthbert Whiteside (*see also p. 124*), with the spade, was to be shot down and killed over France in December 1916 by Mannfred von Richthofen, the legendary German fighter pilot, the Red Baron.

Samuel Davidson (knighted in 1921) operates the hand howitzer which he developed for use in the First World War, and which could discharge grenades or fragmentation shells up to 300 yards. Davidson's establishment of Sirocco Works (*see picture on p. 8*) in 1881 owed much to his inventive mind – initially with tea-drying machinery for the trade in India.

372 Cregagh Road. Now a doctor's surgery, this is 'Rubicon', the family home of Private William McFadzean who sacrificed his own life to save those of many of his comrades on the morning of 1 July 1916. For his selfless courage at Thiepval Wood he was awarded the Victoria Cross.

The Campbell College War Memorial, inaugurated in 1923 by General Alexander Godley, contains the names of the 594 pupils who volunteered during the First World War. Those from East Belfast include C.S. Lewis from 'Little Lea' (*see photograph on p. 39*), the future Baron MacDermott and W.J. English VC (*see photograph on p. 59*). The central panel displays the names of 126 pupils who were killed in the conflict. The statues were carved by the Holywood sculptress, Rosamund Praeger.

Capt. James S. Davidson (1877-1916). After attending school at Inst, Davidson received commercial training at Campbell College (1894-95). He became a director and general manager at his father's Sirocco Works. In the First World War he became a captain in the 13th Battalion, Royal Irish Rifles (36th Division), and was killed in action on the first day of the Battle of the Somme (1 July 1916). His name appears on the Thiepval Memorial, but his body lies in Serre Road No 2 Cemetery.

2nd Lieut. Robin MacDermott (1890-1916). One of three sons of Rev John MacDermott, minister of Belmont Presbyterian Church (*see photograph on p.* 88), he interrupted his legal studies and enlisted in the 8th Battalion (East Belfast), Royal Irish Rifles. He was the first officer of the Ulster Division to be killed, and is buried in Auchonvillers Military Cemetery. His younger brother was Baron Clarke MacDermott, Lord Chief Justice of Northern Ireland (1951-1971).

War Memorial, Somme estate. The houses on this Cregagh estate (*see photograph on p. 44*) were built after the First World War for returning servicemen. This central memorial is built in the shape of a Celtic cross, a common design at the time, and was inaugurated in November 1932 by HRH The Prince of Wales.

Campbell College pupils practise air-raid precautions, *c.* 1939. The shelters were specially constructed at the rear of the school.

ARP post 417 situated in Mountpottinger RUC station.

Willowfield ARP, *c.* 1940. This post was situated in a corner shop at the Euston Street/ Willowfield Street junction. It includes: Thomas and Norman McDowell (fourth and first right, back row); second row: Mr Holywell Jnr (third from left), Eric Blaney (third from right) and Mr Harvey (extreme right); front row: William Ranson, the Post Warden (second left), Mr William Hutton, the District Warden, and his wife (third and fourth left), William Lowry and Mr Holywell Snr (fourth and second right).

Bomb damage to No 24 General Hospital in Campbell College, whose pupils had been evacuated to the Northern Counties Hotel, Portrush. The hospital was bombed by the Luftwaffe on the night of 4-5 May 1941. This picture shows damage to the north-wing roof. One of those prematurely discharged as a result of this attack was the Ulster writer, Sam McAughtry. (IWM: H9482)

Further damage to No 24 General Hospital. Nissen huts were erected in the grounds as wards. A number at the rear were seriously damaged in the raid, and 19 doctors and patients were killed. C.S. Lewis wrote to a local friend, Arthur Greeves: 'It's like the end of the world to think of bombs near Schomberg [an adjacent estate]'. (IWM: H9480)

Entertaining the troops, *c.* 1941. A group of children (*see front cover*) entertain soldiers at New Road School, Newtownards Road, on the site of the present Constitution Club. Mrs Murray sits amongst the men. Robert Paterson sits at the right-hand end of the second row.

William John English VC received the Victoria Cross for gallantry in person from King Edward VII in July 1901 during the Boer War. He lived at 10 King's Road, and died on active service in 1941.

Ravenscroft Avenue after the Blitz. This district was hit in the first wave of German bombing in mid-April 1941. Ravenscroft Public Elementary School was towards the centre left of the picture!

Five
The Corner Shop

Black's general store in Fraser Street (Newtownards Road). No 63 remained until 1979 by which time the rest of the street had been demolished.

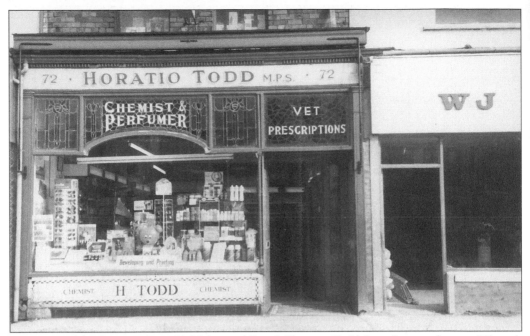

Horatio Todd's chemist shop, 72 Holywood Road. Horatio Todd (*see photograph on p. 30*) took over from another chemist (Perrot & Co.) on this site in 1906, and became almost a legend. Todd's still exists, although altered.

The Castle Inn, Beersbridge Road. On the junction with Kenbaan Street, this building was erected in the 1890s. It became the Bunch of Grapes in the late 1950s, then changed its name to The Castle Inn. It reverted to its previous name in 1991.

Derelict shoemaker's premises, 11 October 1937. This photograph was taken on the opposite corner of the street in the picture on the lower right opposite (Beersbridge Road/Kenbaan Street).

The Farmer's Rest, 108 Castlereagh Street. Built in the 1870s, it acquired the name in 1890, as a result of the fact that farmers called in to sell their produce. The MacMahon family owned it between 1911 and 1970. In 1939 they bought No 106 from Jordan's hairdressers (*see photograph below*), who moved to No 104. It was in recent years owned by the Glentoran and Linfield footballer, Warren Feeney.

Jordan's hairdressers. Robert Jordan, seen in the photograph, had been at No 106 Castlereagh Street since 1921 (taking over from Henry O'Neill) when he moved next-door in 1939. He retired in 1961 and these premises were also purchased by The Farmer's Rest.

Shops at the top of Templemore Avenue. This row of shops dated back to 1896. When photographed in the late 1970s it included a fruit shop and a gents' hairdressers, but has now been completely demolished.

Mary McKibben outside her shop, White Row, Ravenhill Road. This was more usually known as Carrie Dunn's shop. In his autobiography, Rowel Friers recalled: 'At the end of the row and near the corner of Shamrock Street was Carrie Dunn's shop. It was a shop where you could get almost anything you needed ... Carrie's knowledge of local gossip was comprehensive ... and was free with every purchase' (*see also photograph on p. 14*).

Two views of James Hanna's shops. James Hanna first had a shop at 21 Medway Street in 1924. He moved to 88 Dee Street (the lower picture) in 1930, and then about 1935 he established a store at 59a Island Street (probably the upper picture).

Originally called Davidson and Ledlie's, this well-known landmark at Mountpottinger Corner became Davidson and Murray's in the 1890s. It remained there until the early 1960s.

The "D. & M." Spectacles can be depended on for ACCURACY, COMFORT AND STYLE.

DAVIDSON & MURRAY *Ltd.*

MOUNTPOTTINGER CORNER, BELFAST

HEALTH INSURANCE CHEMISTS & OPTICIANS

TELEPHONE 1273

THE CORNER FOR MEDICINE, GLASSES AND SURGICAL APPLIANCES.

Harper's shop was located at 149a Beersbridge Road from 1944 until the late 1980s.

The interior of Magee's chemist shop on the Albertbridge Road.

Peden's hardware shop. Succeeding another hardware merchant, Thomas Peden had a shop at 99 Albertbridge Road from 1932 until 1970.

Pawnbrokers on the Albertbridge Road. There has been a pawnbroker's shop at 224-26 Albertbridge Road from at least 1918. The current occupants, since 1962, are G. & J. Geddis, who are also gents' outfitters. They succeeded Alldritt & Co., who had taken over from Harper, Quinn & Co. in 1952.

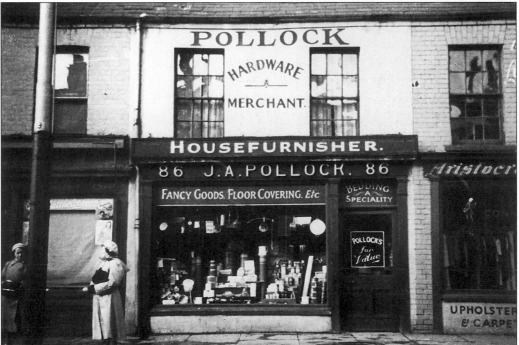

Pollock's for Value. J.A. Pollock traded at 86 Albertbridge Road from 1915 for just over forty years.

This was the first outlet of Russell Wine Cellars at the Ardgowan Street/Woodstock Road junction. It was redesigned after bomb damage in the 1980s. The three houses to the right were also purchased from the Church of Ireland, and now form The Eastender restaurant.

Griffin's hairdressers, which stood at No 130 on the bend of the Woodstock Road, operated for thirty-five years from the end of the Second World War. Note the scrolled pillar decoration.

A veritable farmyard of carcasses adorns McIldoon's butcher's (or flesher's) shop at 30 Woodstock Street (off Albertbridge Road). The shop traded here for over fifty years from 1890.

Elliott Bew, who lived in Hawthornden Road, was – as the sign proclaims – the 'sole Irish representative' of Farmiloe Paints, based at 1 Oxford Street from the late 1930s.

Houston's corner shop stood at the junction of Frank Street and Stormount Street. The building dated back to at least 1884, but had disappeared by the late 1970s.

Tommy Millar, on right, stands outside his hairdressing salon, which is believed to have been at the bottom of Newtownards Road. Tommy also groomed the recently-departed for funerals!

Beattie's corner shop in Grace Avenue, Bloomfield.

Abernethy's chemists was originally at 232 and 234 Albertbridge Road in the early years of this century, but had moved to No 230 by the early 1920s (*see photograph on p. 74*). This business, started by Campbell Blakey Abernethy in 1890, was originally a druggist and grocery shop. Abernethy lived at 'Lismoyne' on the Upper Newtownards Road near Knock junction.

The interior of Abernethy's chemists. Mrs Cora Watson, on the left in the photograph, is the founder's granddaughter. The company celebrated its centenary on the last day of 1990, but had closed down by 1994.

S.D. Bell's at Knock Corner. It is unfair to call Bell's a corner-shop. It is a long-established company with a branch here since the late 1930s, which still produces its own-brand tea and coffee. The scene has changed quite dramatically in the last twenty years; the Northern Bank is now housed in what was, when built, quite an avant-garde building.

Six
Education

St Matthew's Primary School, Seaforde Street (1902-1994). This developed from an earlier one-storey school which opened in February 1846.

The old Newtownards Road Methodist School, 1892, which was also known as Belvoir National School, as it was close to Belvoir Street. The schoolmaster was Mr W.J. Currie, and the schoolmistress was Miss McClelland. The boy at the right-hand end of the second row is David Kirkpatrick, later a master painter.

Bill's School. This school, built on the Beersbridge Road in 1865, was named after its best-known headmaster, James Bill. It educated workers in the Grove Spinning Mill (on Grove Street East). After various other uses, it is presently used by the Dyke Senior Citizens' Club.

Harding Memorial School, Cregagh Road. This was originally called Willowfield No 2 National School, and was renamed in 1922 (*see photograph on p. 38*).

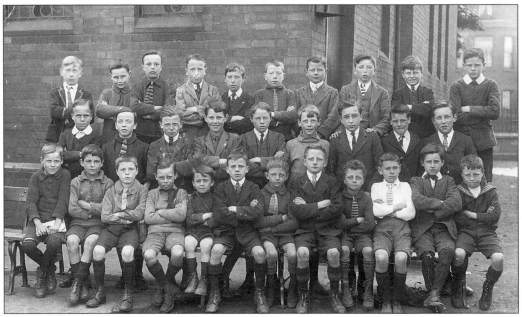

St Donard's School, Bloomfield Road, *c.* 1920. In the back row (fifth from left) is Billy Gillespie, and two to his right is a boy called Weir.

Campbell College, 1917. The headmaster was Robert McFarland known as 'Billy'. One pupil, the future Prof. E.R. Dodds, described him as 'a fat man ... whose superfluous flesh quivered like a jelly'. Some of the pupils shown here include Frederick Mitchell (third row from back, eleventh from left), Bishop of Down & Dromore; and in the back row: George Buchanan (second from left), writer and poet; Miles Delap (tenth from left), who won the DFC in 1940; and William Fraser Browne (sixth from right), a future Irish rugby international. Seated amongst the young boys on the front row are: William MacQuitty (second from the left),

producer of the film about the 'Titanic', *A Night to Remember*; J.S. Fairley, Professor of Zoology at Galway, and F.E. McKeever, Irish champion jockey (1933) and winner of two Irish Grand Nationals (seventh and eighth from the right); and William McCalla (twelfth from the left), founder of the McCalla Travel Agency and winner of the Co. Down (motor-racing) Trophy in 1934. The trophy in front of the headmaster is the Schools' Cup, the oldest rugby trophy in Ireland, which Campbell has won 25 times.

Tullycarnet National School, founded in 1839, which stood on the right of King's Road, on the way to Dundonald.

Ledley Hall on Lord Street. It was founded in 1897 by a director of Bank Buildings, and remained an educational establishment until 1937. During the Second World War it was briefly a fire station, and then it became a youth club before demolition in the 1980s.

Strandtown National School, Dundela Street. The principal from 1898 to 1916 was William Slator, on the right, (*see photograph on p. 37*). The female teacher in front of him is probably his wife.

Strandtown Public Elementary School, 1934. By the 1930s Strandtown School had moved to new premises on North Road. The pupils in Standards 7 and 8 are shown with vice-principal William Cowan.

Belmont Public Elementary School, 1925. On the Belmont Road, this was originally called Ferguson Memorial School. From left to right, back row: -?-, Frances Milligan, Addie Abbott, Rhoda Cupples, Bessie Connery, Stella Davis, Millie Laughlin and Doreen Couser; in front of them: Norah Cathcart, Maisie Wilson, Elsie Hanna, Lily McAvoy, Sheila McCormick, Ruby Heatherington, Miss Kerr, Hannah McClure, Helen McPherson, Sheila Couser, Miss Harrison and Dorothy Whillan; standing in the second row back: Florrie Wilson, Kath Ward, Winnie Bell, Yvonne Wilson, Dorothy Wright, Peggy McBurney, Hetty Thompson and Miss Napier; seated: Nellie Hay, Nancy Hewitt, Elsie Liggett, Doreen Bowes, Helen Smyth, Bea Mussom, Pansy Whiteside, May Livingstone, Lizzie Geary and Mavis Scott.

Seven
Church and Mission

Willowfield parish church was designed by John Lanyon and consecrated in 1872. It is pictured above before its extension in 1901. The spire has been dismantled twice (1912 and 1951). Willowfield's No 1 National School opened in 1884 on the Woodstock Road, closed in 1927, and is currently the surgery of Drs Miller and Little. The building in the background was then the post office, and is now Little's menswear shop.

McQuiston Memorial (Presbyterian) Church opened in the early 1890s. Rev T.R. Ballantine was minister from 1893 to 1910 before leaving for the Transvaal.

Pitt Street (Methodist) Choir at the end of the First World War. The only known person pictured is Ginnie McAnally (third from the left in the front row). Pitt Street formed the 39th Boys Brigade (*see photograph on p. 122*).

The temporary premises on the Cregagh Road before the building of the current Cregagh Presbyterian Church in 1928.

At the junction of Belmont Road/Dundela Street, opposite Gelston's Corner, this was the first St Mark's parish church opened in 1863. After the church moved along the Holywood Road (1878) this building became Strandtown National School, whose principal at the turn of the century was William Slator (*see photograph on p. 37*). In recent years the site has been occupied by Stewart's supermarket.

One of the thirty Belfast City mission halls in a state of dereliction in East Belfast.

Skipton Street Baptist Mission Hall dated from the late nineteenth century, and was referred to in 1899 as a Working Men's Mission Hall.

The Foundry Street Mission Hall was located at 86-88 Foundry Street from the late 1910s until 1973. The presence of so many mission halls in East Belfast is probably a sign of the hardship and deprivation which accompanied the industrialisation of the district.

The Belfast City Mission Church at Lord Street at the junction with Haig Street. It was built about 1918.

The interior of St John's Church, Laganbank, the exterior of which can be seen on page 23. The church has now been demolished and a new one was built at the top of Castlereagh Road in the late 1950s.

The site for a church, manse and school for Belmont Presbyterian Church on Sydenham Avenue was offered by Sir Thomas McClure (*see photograph on p. 24*). It opened in January 1862. The manse is to the left, and the house in the middle was occupied by Mr H.C. Craig.

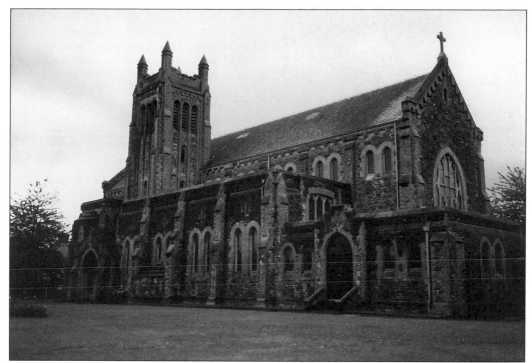

St Anthony's Chapel, Willowfield. A boys' school, opened in 1913, was attached to this church in Willowfield Drive, until alterations were made to the building in 1970.

First Ballymacarrett Presbyterian Church. This was the original building, close to Paulett Avenue, which was inaugurated in 1837, because of the growth in the number of Presbyterians in the district, which left '1,500 persons without the superintendence of a Christian pastor'.

The date of foundation on Castlereagh Presbyterian Church in Church Road is 1650, but this building was erected in 1834, seating 800. It was the first Presbyterian church in Ireland to boast a tower.

Repairs being carried out to Mountpottinger Baptist Tabernacle. The foundation stone was laid on 17 September 1892. There were at this point only two Baptist churches in Belfast, but nearly 600 worshippers in East Belfast without a church.

Eight
Industry and Transport

The staff at the Sirocco Works head office, 19 October 1912. Seated on the front row are a number of directors: G.W. Matthew, F.G. Maguire, Samuel C. Davidson (founder), James Inglis (President, American Blower Co.), James Davidson (General Manager – *see photograph on p. 55*) and G.G. Ward.

Bloomfield railway station, Beersbridge Road, was part of the Belfast & County Down Railway before demolition in 1948.

Knock station was a little further along the line, close to where the RUC headquarters is now located.

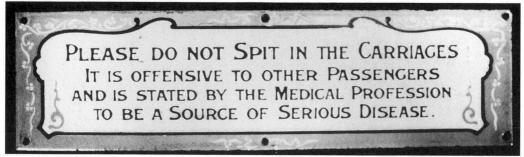

PLEASE DO NOT SPIT IN THE CARRIAGES
IT IS OFFENSIVE TO OTHER PASSENGERS
AND IS STATED BY THE MEDICAL PROFESSION
TO BE A SOURCE OF SERIOUS DISEASE.

The 'Do not spit' request appeared in railway carriages. Spitting was one of the ways by which tuberculosis – particularly virulent in Ireland – was transmitted. One of those who did most to tackle tuberculosis before the Second World War was Dr Brice Clarke of Forster Green and Whiteabbey hospitals.

John Gray, left, and two colleagues in the railway repair yards before the Second World War.

William Smith, the proprietor, seated, centre, and staff in the late 1940s at the Cregagh Dairies (*see also photograph on p. 32*), which were at Loopland Drive from 1945 to 1970. Also seated, extreme right, is William's brother Herbert. Standing are Victor Smith, second left, and Norman Russell, third right.

Lamplighters at the Albertbridge Road depot, 25 February 1936. One lamplighter, W.J. Mercer of Belmont Road, served nearly fifty years from 1897. He started on 13s 6d for a seven-day week.

Above the workers' entrance in Cluan Place, Musgrave Foundry displayed the coat of arms of the Prince of Wales, one of their customers. Founded in the 1850s, its main works – originally producing ventilating equipment – were located off the Albertbridge Road from 1893 until 1965. Another customer was Monsieur Eiffel of 'Tower' fame.

The Loopbridge Mill, off the Castlereagh Road, was originally used for spinning. In 1893 it was taken over by McCaw, Stevenson & Orr, printers.

An overview of the Belfast Ropeworks at Connswater probably *c*. 1930.

A delivery, probably from the Belfast Ropeworks, comes down the Albertbridge Road (at Mountpottinger corner – *see photograph on p. 17*) in the early years of this century.

No 1 Manila Preparing Department, Belfast Ropeworks, 7 January 1935.

No 2 Manila Preparing Department, Belfast Ropeworks, 17 January 1935.

A Belfast Ropeworks annual outing, probably in the 1920s.

A Ropeworks cart carrying Blue-Bell binder twine.

The balling department in the Ropeworks' Bloomfield factory manufacturing balls of string.

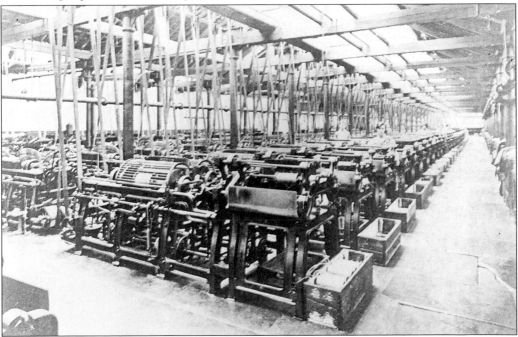

Ropeworks' twisting machines. Belfast Ropeworks, founded in 1880, survived over one hundred years and was, at one stage, the largest in the world.

A steam shovel prepares the foundations for Stormont Parliament, April 1924.

The façade at Stormont begins to take shape, late 1920s.

The men of the Belfast Tramways at the Mountpottinger Depot in 1944.

The men of the Tramways photographed near the Knock Depot (*see the photographs on p. 22*). They donned the white caps on 1 May each year.

A Sirocco Tea retail van about the time of the First World War.

Queen's Bridge being prepared for the tramways. The Albert Clock is in the distance.

Two men take a break at the coal-yards near the docks. They were paid 4*d* per ton for filling bags manually for household delivery – and breaks were unpaid!

At the coal-yards Bertie and Jack Boyd take advantage of mechanisation which was installed in the late 1950s.

In the early decades of its development, there were many brickworks in East Belfast, along the banks of the Lagan and inland. This old brickyard was at Lead Hill, just off the current junction of the Ring Road and Ballygowan Road.

The BP Oil Refinery in Belfast Lough, photographed in 1964. Holywood is in the background.

Harland & Wolff's timekeeping and wages staff, *c.* 1953. William Hutton is on the far left. The man standing, second from the right, was Billy Couser, who was the pianist with a four-piece band which accompanied silent films at the original Princess picture-house which closed in 1923.

Derek Bolton, an iron-turner at Harland & Wolff.

Harland & Wolff's boiler shop workers (2pm to 10pm shift), 19 June 1935.

Samson and Goliath were built in the 1960s to service Harland & Wolff. Here one of them works on the *Esso Ulidia*.

The Duke of Lancaster passenger ferry in Belfast Docks in the days when there was a ferry from Liverpool to Belfast.

Short Brothers originally moved from Battersea to East Belfast in 1932. Here one of their guided weapons' engineers, Jack McBride, tests the new supersonic anti-aircraft missile, the 'Blowpipe', September 1968.

Weighing bonded tobacco at Gallaher's Connswater warehouse, November 1960.

An aerial view of the Gallaher Connswater warehouse, 1949. This part of the Gallaher company opened in Severn Street in August 1936. The Oval can just be seen at the top left of the picture.

Nine

Buildings

'Craigavon' on Circular Road was the family home of Sir James Craig, the first prime minister of Northern Ireland. It was here that Craig and his supporters planned a provisional government in 1913 in case Home Rule became law. In later years it became the Somme Hospital for veterans of the 36th (Ulster) Division, and is now the offices of the Somme Association.

An idealised architect's view of the Ulster Hospital for Children and Women in Templemore Avenue, founded in 1872. The existing building does not possess the sloping roofs.

Ulster Bank House on the Albertbridge Road was built in the 1920s on the junction with Cluan Place.

Built of red-brick in the mid-1890s, 195 Templemore Avenue may have started life as one of the more fashionable town houses of the district. However, much of its recent use has been devoted to official (often Health Department) purposes. Templemore Avenue was designed in the early 19th century as part of a plan of urban development, built on the grid system typical of French or American cities.

The fire station at 355 Albertbridge Road finally closed down at the end of the 1960s. The building, photographed here in the 1980s, has since been demolished.

Albertbridge Road Orange Hall was built in 1901. It is of rather hybrid design with an ornate entrance porch.

The former
entrance to St
Ann's Works, the
Spence Bryson
goods' entry in
Cluan Place.

The former Knock Tramway Depot (*see photographs on p. 101*) opposite S.D. Bell's.

The former Avoniel Distillery which occupied the site of the old Connswater Spinning Mill from 1882. It depended very much upon sources of artesian water.

Canmer's Building were built in the late 1890s, and occupied a site at the lower end of Newtownards Road until swept away in the construction of the large roundabout at Bridge End.

The old Memel Street Bridge, otherwise known as Fullen's Arch.

An account dating from July 1903 for the decoration of 24 Upper Frank Street. 9s 11d included the 'whiting' of six ceilings and papering the 'parlor'.

The former disinfecting station on the Laganbank Road, 1970s.

No 34 Thorndyke Street, pictured here in the 1970s, once housed the local Girls' Club.

Ten

Leisure

Ravenscroft Public Elementary School (*see p. 60*) football team, 1938-39, with Mr Rodgers, the principal, and Mr Thompson at the rear. Standing, back row: D. Hoey, R. McCallum, J. Masters, R. Murdock and one unknown boy. Seated at the very front: A. Mitchell and M. Masters. The two boys on seats to the left were A. Vine and J. Mitchell; to the right were W. Barton and C. Kelly. In the centre was future Northern Ireland football captain, Danny Blanchflower.

The new stand goes up at the Oval in 1951.

Dundela Football Club (East Belfast), 1924.

Willowfield Football Club 1928, who won the Irish Cup Final against Larne, after a replay.

Orangefield Boys' School Under-15 XI, 1961. Standing: Mr J. Malone, -?-, D. McWilliams, N. Cairns, Anderson, M. McMullan, Mr Thompson Steele. Seated: H. Pickles, J. Shepherd, Roy Coyle, -?-, Eric McMordie. Coyle went on to play for Sheffield Wednesday and McMordie for Middlesborough; both became internationals. Roy Coyle had a very successful period as manager of Linfield, and is now with Ards FC.

The former Willowfield Unionist Club and erstwhile Willowfield picture-house at Woodstock Road/Cherryville Street. This building has now been replaced by a row of modern shop units.

The now-demolished Astoria cinema was located on Upper Newtownards Road for forty years from 1935.

The Popular cinema was at the lower end of Newtownards Road on the corner of Keenan Street from 1917 to 1962. It had a 30-ft screen. Its opening film was *The Ploughshare*, and its last manager was Samuel Bradley. It is drawn here by Jim Patton.

CIYMS Tennis Club, Circular Road, 1946. Seated, with beard, is Sir Milne Barbour. To his left are Gordon Thompson (club captain), Capt. Storey and Albert Smylie. To Barbour's right are Doris Pentland (ladies' captain) and James Thompson. Frank and Eileen Turner are standing at opposite ends of the next row back. Jackie Lamb is third from left.

39th Company Boys' Brigade, Pitt Street, 1912. This company went on to form the 39th Old Boys' Flute Band (*see photographs on pp. 30 and 31*) in 1917. The officers are, from left to right: T.J. Faulkner, W.J. Mackenzie, S.J. Platt, W. Perrott, J. Allen, T. Fleming, D. Paterson, J. Prentice, W. Bolton, J. Shackles, and A. Geddes. During the First World War, S.J. Platt became captain of No 2 Company, 16th Pioneer Battalion of 36th (Ulster) Division, and later worked on the *Yorkshire Post*.

10th Belfast Company Boys' Brigade, Mountpottinger Methodist Church, in the 1930s.

Boys playing marleys (marbles).

A rather staged game of 'churchy-one-man-over'.

Campbell College 1st XV, 1914. Mr Henry Madden, top right, was killed during the First World War which broke out a few weeks after this photograph was taken. Of the fifteen boys shown, seven of them also died: R.E.W. Semple and C.A. Owens (back row, second and third left) also had brothers killed in the war. W.J. Porter (bottom left) helped to organise one of the first daylight raids of the war. G.H. Herriott (middle row, second left) and R.C. Whiteside (middle, centre) were both killed in the war in the air – Whiteside by the Red Baron (*see photograph on p. 52*). G.D. McCullagh and B. Watson (middle row, third and second right) also died. Whiteside and Watson each had a brother killed in the Second World War.

Strand Bowling Club, Victoria Park, taken, according to one elderly man, 'a brave few years ago' – probably the 1960s. Front row, from the left: Mr Russell (first), Hugh Blaney Montgomery (third) and Mr Woods (fifth).

Willowfield or Ormeau Bowling Club, 1940s. Standing at the rear (second right) is Mr White, and (fifth left) Tom Wilson.

Queen's Island XV, Junior Cup finalists, 1932. Sat on the ground are Mr Kyle and Frank Turner, right.

Mersey Street Primary School, *c.* 1960. With Miss F. Cupples, who is pictured top right, are, from left to right, back to front: L. Donovan, S. Nimick, O. Watton, J. Logan, J. Faulkner, G. Millar, Evelyn Dickson, H. Grahame, M. Wilton, M. Dineley, I. Leeman, V. Kingsberry, P. Girvan, L. Dickson and P. Smith.

St Patrick's Church (East Belfast) Silver Band, 1945.

Ravenhill Flute Band, 1937. The conductor was Mr Wallace.

Acknowledgements

As the East Belfast Historical Society possesses a very limited archive, it is very grateful to all those who have helped in the compilation of this volume. Without everyone's assistance and contribution this would have proved an impossible venture.

Particular gratitude is owed to the efforts of Wesley Thompson and Billy Bowden, with much assistance also being offered by John Auld, Thompson Steele, Marion Kelly and Jim Patton. Members of the Society who have contributed include: Billy Cummings, Mrs K. Hamill, William Hutton, Bertha Jones, Norman Kennedy, William Kirkpatrick, Charlie Ludlow, Mrs E. McIlhagga, Joan Pepper, Ruby Purdy, Cecil Slator, Jim Sloan, Frank and Eileen Turner.

Several residents of, or people associated with, East Belfast have also contributed. They are: Desmond Austin, Eileen Beattie, Mr Bell (S.D. Bell's Ltd), Andrene Bolger, Ray Browne (Philip Russell Ltd), Irene Dunwoody, Mrs Gillespie, Henry Hall, Rev Norman Jardine (Willowfield Church of Ireland), Fred Johnson, Reg Jordan, Evelyn Kelleher, Mr F. Kelso, Lorraine Leckey, Michael Lombard (St Matthew's Primary School), Meta Lynar, Norman McDowell, J. and M. McEnally, Edith Mackey, Albert Maxwell, Noel Nesbitt, Joan Nesbitt, Mrs S. Palmer, George Platt, Joan Pollock, Betty Proctor, Doreen Ritchie, Tom Ritchie, Dr and Mrs D. H. Rogers, Peggy Rowe, Alex Scott, Emily Scott, William Smith, J. Stevens, Ruby Thompson, Winifred Thompson, Mrs Warwick (Warwick's), Margaret Wilson, the Misses Wilson and Eric Wright.

The Society is particularly grateful to the following institutions and organisations and their trustees for giving us kind permission to reproduce their material: Campbell College; the Somme Association Ltd (p. 109); the Ordnance Survey (p. 6); R. Yeates and the Belfast Harbour Commissioners (pp. 104, 106, 107); George Woodman and the Assembly Library, Stormont (pp. 36, 100); Bodleian Library: Oxford MS Eng. lett. c. 220/2, fol. 14r (p. 35); the Imperial War Museum, London (Crown Copyright, IWM) (p. 58); the Ulster Folk and Transport Museum (pp. 17, 100); the Deputy Keeper of the Public Records of Northern Ireland & Sirocco Company (pp. 11, 53, 91); the Ulster Museum (pp. 2, 7, 18, 19, 23, 24, 60, 63).

Unfortunately, I have been unable to trace the anonymous donor who provided the front cover. It shows a group of schoolchildren, apparently from New Road School, in Ribble Street in 1941 collecting scrap metal for the *Belfast Telegraph* Spitfire Appeal. Mrs Murray stands on the left; the boy giving the 'thumbs up' sign is Robert Paterson, who died in Fiji in the late 1980s.